A "Read, America!" Classic

The How Rude!™ Handbook of

Family Manners
for Teens

Avoiding Strife in Family Life

The How Rude! Handbook of

Family Manners for Teens

Avoiding Strife in Family Life

Alex J. Packer, Ph.D.

Edited by Pamela Espeland

free spirit
PUBLiSHiNG®

Helping kids
help themselves™
since 1983

CAUTION!

This is a book about manners.

If that makes you feel like throwing up, at least say "Excuse me" before rushing to the bathroom.

INTRODUCTION

Do any of these sound like you?

"I hate you!"
"You can't make me."
"Whatever."
"@*$%& you!!!"

Do any of these sound like your parents*?

"Shut up!"
"Because I said so."
"Why did I ever have kids?"
"@*$%& you!!!"

Belonging to a family means you all have a place where you can be yourselves. Your best selves—and your worst selves.

You can brag, cry, and complain. You can be silly and moody, dreamy and weird. You can break a promise, tell a

---

* In this book, "parents" means biological parents. Or adoptive parents. Or stepparents. Or foster parents. Or any other adults you live with who take care of you. It can even mean one parent. If you're part of a blended, shaken, stirred, or extended family, you might want to turn to page 75 right away.

fib, and slam a door. You can shout, "I wish I was never born!" and know that your parents will still love you.

At home, in our families, we don't call this "rudeness." We call it "growing up." That's why mistakes, tantrums, and hurtful words are usually forgiven.

But some people think it's *always* okay to say and do what you want at home. You *never* have to be polite or kind. They call this "being honest." Instead, it can be selfish, mean, and rude.

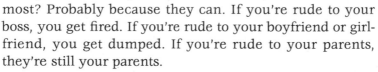

Some parents and kids *enjoy* making each other feel sad or mad. And that's too bad.

Why do people behave so rudely to those they care about most? Probably because they can. If you're rude to your boss, you get fired. If you're rude to your boyfriend or girl-friend, you get dumped. If you're rude to your parents, they're still your parents.

You spend more time with your family than just about anyone else. Home should be the place where you feel safe, loved, relaxed, and accepted. It should be the place where you know you'll be treated with kindness and under-standing. It should be the place where you practice your *best*, not worst, manners.

This book covers the basics of good manners at home. It doesn't deal with every possible family type or situation. No book can do that. But it covers enough that you're sure to find something here for you. Ideas to think about. Sugges-tions to try. And ways to make family life better for everyone.

Why Manners Matter

Maybe you're thinking, "Nobody's polite anymore. Why should I be?" Or, "Who cares about manners?" Or, "The world is getting ruder every day. Why not join the crowd?"

The truth is, bad manners hurt everyone. And good manners help everyone, including you.

When you have good manners, you know how to act in all kinds of situations. You know the right things to say and do. You're confident, calm, and cool.

10 Ways Having Good Manners Can Help You

1. **Good manners put other people at ease.** People at ease are more likely to agree when you ask them for something.

2. **Good manners impress people.** People who are impressed by your behavior are more likely to treat you with respect.

3. **Good manners build self-esteem.** Teens with self-esteem are more likely to get what they want out of life.

4. **Good manners make you look good.** People like being around thoughtful, polite kids.

5. **Good manners help people live and work together more easily.** This makes your world more pleasant.

6. **Good manners can keep you out of trouble.** You're less likely to disrespect people and get hurt.

continues...

7. **Good manners set you apart.** Because they're so rare, teens who have them sparkle like diamonds.

8. **Good manners make you feel good.** You're doing your part to save society from a total manners meltdown.

9. **Good manners make others feel good.** You can help to create a world in which people treat one another with care, respect, and compassion.

10. **Good manners don't cost anything.** You can have the BEST for free.

Most teens want to have good manners. When we did a survey of teens, 93 percent agreed with this statement: "It's important to have good manners."

Why? Here are some of the reasons they gave:

"It's a way of respecting yourself."
"People will like you better."
"I want to make good first impressions with people."
"The way you act is the way you get treated."
"Being polite feels better than being rude."

And here are some ways good manners helped the teens in our survey:

"I got a job."
"I got something I wanted from my parents."
"I got compliments and respect."

"I got in good with the opposite sex."

"I got help from teachers."

So good manners aren't just for company anymore. They're for anyone who wants to get along, get noticed, and get ahead.

How to Use This Book

Read the parts that interest you. Try the ideas that make sense to you. Are you looking for a specific tip or topic? Skim the Contents and the Index to save time and zero in on what you want and need.

This book is all about you. Your actions. Your behaviors. Your words. Your attitudes. Your manners. You can't make other people polite, but you can make yourself the kind of person that people like, respect, and enjoy being around.

Good luck—and good manners!

Alex Packer
Boston, Massachusetts

Why are manners so important? Isn't it what's inside a person that counts?

Of course. But nobody's going to want to know the "real you" if you gross them out. ◆

The Basics
of Family Harmony

A lot of people think there are two kinds of manners: *company manners* and *everyday manners.*

One is for show, and one is for family. The one for show is the phony you, and the one for family is the real you. Being polite is phony. Being sloppy and gross is real.

Where did we get the idea that our real selves are disgusting slobs?

It's okay to relax a bit when company isn't around. But we should strive to be less formal, not more rude.

In other words, it's okay to bring the ketchup bottle to the table. But it's not okay to ask for it without saying "please." It's okay to tell jokes and be silly. But it's not okay to burp the ABCs and stick straws up your nose.

The 10 Rudest Things Teens Do at Home

• •

When we asked adults, "What are the rudest things teens do at home?" these were the top 10 answers:

1. Interrupt other people's conversations.
2. Not say "Please" or "Thank you."
3. Wear hats at the table.
4. Throw their backpacks and jackets on the floor.
5. Talk back.
6. Use vulgar language (swear).
7. Act mean to their siblings.
8. Be rude on the telephone.
9. Say "Yeah" or "Uh-huh" instead of "Yes."
10. Whine.

Daily Do's

In most homes, there are adults who do the cooking, cleaning, laundry, driving, bill-paying, and child-raising. They are usually called "Mom" and "Dad." Here's how to be on good terms with yours, along with other family members:

ACKNOWLEDGE THEIR PRESENCE. You don't have to say, "Hi, how are you? What's new?" each time you run into a family member at home. But it's nice to say "Good morning" and "Good night." In between, talk to them in ways that show you care about them and their lives. Don't just ignore them or go whole days without saying a word.

TUNE INTO THEIR MOODS. If your own moods go up and down faster than a speeding yo-yo, you know that sometimes people need to be left alone. And sometimes they want company or a helping hand. If family members seem upset, say, "You seem kind of (sad, unhappy, stressed out) today. Is there anything I can do?" If they want to talk, they will. If they don't, they will still appreciate your reaching out and being kind.

WATCH YOUR TIMING. If your brother just broke up with his girlfriend, it's not a good time to tease him. If your mom just got a raise, it is a good time to ask for a bigger allowance. Adjust your requests and behavior to the feelings and needs of others. This is one way to be polite. It's also a way to improve your chances of getting what you want.

TALK TO THEM. For some strange reason, parents believe they have the right to know what's going on in their kids' lives. That's why this kind of conversation drives them crazy:

> Parent: *"What did you do in school today?"*
> Teen: *"Nothin'."*
> Parent: *"Who was that you were talking with?"*
> Teen: *"Nobody."*
> Parent: *"What are your plans for this evening?"*
> Teen: *"I dunno."*

One of the most polite things you can do for your parents is talk to them. Maybe you already do. Maybe your parents are the first people you think of when you have news to share and problems to sort out. If so, keep it up. But if you never or hardly ever talk to your parents, they probably feel hurt and ignored.

Here are two ways to change that for the better:

1. **Tell them things.** Tell them what went on at school, what you're thinking, and how you're feeling. You don't have to get deeply personal or go into a lot of detail. Just share stuff about classes, teachers, other kids, plans, your reactions to current events, etc.

2. **Ask them things.** Ask them about their work, friends, and interests. Ask them about their childhood. *Examples:* "How did work go today?" "Did you have a good time at dinner with the Flugelhorns last night?" "What kind of student were you in high school?" "What did you like to do when you were my age?" "How did you get along with Grandma and Grandpa back then?" The list is endless. In fact, one well-chosen question such as, "Dad, what was it like growing up on military bases and moving all the time?" can keep your father talking for half an hour or longer. He won't notice that he's doing all the talking. He'll appreciate your interest and feel a warm glow from spending quality time with you. (**TIP:** When you ask people questions about themselves, they usually think you're a great conversationalist.)

BRING THINGS UP BEFORE THEY TURN INTO PROBLEMS.
Many family arguments and misunderstandings can be
avoided by thinking ahead. *Examples:* Don't wait until the
last minute to ask for a ride to the mall. Don't wait until the
night before to tell your mom you volunteered her to bake
400 brownies for a school fair. (**TIP:** Don't ever volunteer a
parent to do *anything* without checking with him or her first.)

10 Polite Things Parents Wish Teens Would Do

When we asked adults, "Which good manners would you most like
your kids to use?" these were the top 10 answers:

1. Say "Please," "Thank you," "You're welcome," "May I...?" and
   "Excuse me."

2. Write thank-you notes.

3. Look people in the eye.

4. Clean up after themselves.

5. Respect adults.

6. Not interrupt—wait for their turn to speak.

7. Treat people as they would like to be treated.

8. Use good table manners.

9. Give people a firm handshake.

10. Have compassion toward others.

Bonus Behaviors

Here are four easy ways to earn extra politeness points:

LET YOUR PARENTS KNOW WHERE YOU ARE. If they expect you home from school at 3:00 every day, they'll worry if you haven't shown up by 3:30. Leave a note if you plan to be late, or a phone message if you know you'll be late.

SMILE ONCE IN A WHILE. A scowling teenager is a dark cloud in the family sky. True, adolescence has its gloomy days. But if life generally treats you well, why not wear a pleasant expression?

PICK UP AFTER YOURSELF. Parents *hate it* when kids drop their belongings all over the house. If you're ever kidnapped, try to leave a trail. Otherwise, close doors, shut drawers, wipe off, pick up, put away, take back, and clear off as required.

DO THINGS WITHOUT BEING ASKED OR TOLD. Say, "Mom, let me hold that for you." Or, "Dad, do you want me to take out the recycling?" If a faucet is running, turn it off. If car windows are open in the rain, close them. If the trash is overflowing, tie up the bag and replace it with a new one. These thoughtful gestures will do wonders for your standing at home.

Should my mom barge into my room without knocking?

No, and you shouldn't barge into hers. Respecting each other's privacy is not just polite. It's also smart. There are some things you simply don't want to see each other doing. Ask your mom to knock and wait for a "Come in" before entering your room. Promise to do the same for her. ◆

50 COMMANDMENTS
OF FAMILY ETIQUETTE

THOU SHALT...

1. respect each other

2. do your part to keep the house neat

3. say "Please" and "Thank you"

4. be polite when answering the phone and door

5. use proper table manners

6. disagree without being disagreeable

7. ask without yelling

8. listen attentively

9. clean up after yourself

10. keep your room tidy

11. turn down the volume on the TV and stereo when asked

12. be willing to compromise

13. treat others as you would like to be treated

14. share willingly

15. clean up the house after your friends leave

16. treat each other's property with care and respect

17. apologize sincerely when apologies are called for

18. rejoice in each other's successes

50 COMMANDMENTS
OF FAMILY ETIQUETTE

19. empathize with each other's pain

20. put your dirty clothes in the hamper

21. recognize your own contributions to family squabbles

22. be thoughtful of each other—especially if you know a family member is having a hard day

23. turn off the TV when company is over

24. take responsibility for your own actions and words

25. smile

THOU SHALT NOT...

26. lie

27. hit

28. snoop

29. whine

30. interrupt

31. use crude language

32. accept phone calls during family meal times

33. open a closed door without first knocking—and waiting to be invited in

34. take each other's belongings without first asking

continues...

50 COMMANDMENTS
OF FAMILY ETIQUETTE

35. tell each other's secrets

36. leave your sports and exercise equipment in the hall

37. ignore each other's requests

38. be afraid to speak up when you feel something is wrong

39. pass each other first thing in the day without saying good morning, or last thing at night without saying good night

40. throw your jackets, hats, and shoes all over the house

41. spend all day or night on the telephone or the computer

42. forget to take out the trash

43. embarrass family members in front of their friends

44. take money from each other's wallets without asking

45. schedule commitments for each other without clearing them in advance

46. drop your clothes on the floor

47. leave dirty dishes all over the house

48. forget to do your chores

49. read each other's mail

50. treat each other rudely

Around the House

If you want to see Manners Gone Wild, step into the family room, kitchen, or bathroom of the typical household. The way family members quibble, nibble, and dribble can be a recipe for disaster.

"Who trashed my DVD?"

"Who used my razor?"

"Who spilled something sticky on the floor?"

"Why can't I wear boxers around the house?"

"Meatloaf AGAIN?!"

As a well-mannered teen, you can do your part to keep family life from being a free-for-all. Read on to learn how.

TV Civility

The invention of the remote-controlled television brought about a new era in TV watching. Viewers no longer had to get up and walk across the room to change channels, or sit through commercials.

The remote also led to a new type of vegetable: the couch potato. And it created a new subject for family fights and arguments: Who controls the remote.

"Whenever we watch TV as a family, my brother grabs the remote. Every time there's a commercial, he starts flipping through the channels. Then he'll see something he likes, usually sports, and everyone has to start yelling, 'Change back, change back,' and by the time he does, we've missed some of the program we were watching and everyone's in a bad mood."

In every family, one person usually acts as the Keeper of the Remote. Ideally, he or she won't be a dictator or a hog. Instead, that person will honor the responsibilities of that role. These include:

- adjusting the volume to an acceptable level

- changing (or not changing) channels, based on the wishes of the majority, and

- leaving the remote in a convenient location so the next person to watch TV won't have to spend three hours looking for it

Brothers who abuse their power should be sat on by the rest of the family until they hand over the remote or agree to use it according to the wishes of the majority. Parents who turn into TV tyrants should be invited to a family meeting to discuss this issue.

But there's more to polite TV watching than controlling the remote. Like:

CHOOSING WHAT TO WATCH. This is done by vote ("All those in favor of *Wall Street Week,* raise your hand"), alternation ("I decide tonight, you decide tomorrow"), or decree ("Because I'm the parent, that's why!"). Multi-TV households can cut down on these conflicts. So can those with VCRs or DVRs—simply record one show while you're watching another.

TALKING. The family TV room is not a movie theater, so talking during TV viewing is usually allowed. Often, this consists of sparkling commentary followed by a chorus of "Shut ups!"

The typical family includes many different personality types. They are easily identified by the remarks they make while watching TV:

■ *The Scornful One:* "The whole space station is nothing but a bunch of crummy miniatures."

■ *The Picky One:* "That's so lame. He just fired eight shots when that gun only holds six."

■ *The Spacey One:* "Are we going to the outlet mall this weekend?"

■ *The Clueless One:* "Is that the same woman as before? Where are they now? Why did he let her go?"

■ *The Critic:* "The original *Twilight Zone* was way better."

■ *The Spoiler:* "I already saw this movie. The kindergarten teacher did it."

■ *The Cheerleader:* "Yeah! Kill 'em! Blast 'em in the kneecaps!"

■ *The Heckler:* "Where did she learn to act? Who wrote this terrible script? And why did we just see a microphone dangling over their heads?"

■ *The Shusher:* "Sssshhhh!"

KNOWING WHEN TO TURN IT OFF. If your TV is centrally located—in the living room, for example, or the family room—you'll need to agree on some ground rules. Try these for starters:

1. If nobody's watching it, turn it off.

2. If there's nothing good on, turn it off.

3. If company comes, turn it off.

There are two exceptions to rule #3:

1. When someone drops by without being invited or calling first, *and* you're watching something you really want to see, *and* you don't have a VCR or DVR, you can say, "Oh, hi! We're all watching the NASCAR race on TV. Come and join us."

2. When watching TV is the main event and the reason for having company, as on Super Bowl Sunday.

SPOTLIGHT ON...

WHEN YOUR PARENTS WON'T LET YOU WATCH TV

A surprising number of American households are TV-free. That means they don't own a single television. For some strange reason, the parents think they and their kids are better off without TV.

I don't know why those parents are so opposed to television. How else are kids supposed to learn how *not* to act and what *not* to do?

As long as your parents are polite about laying down the law, you have only three choices:

1. You can argue about the educational value of PBS, the History Channel, and the Learning Channel (and hear "Uh-huh").

2. You can throw TV-related tantrums (and hear "Someday you'll thank us for this").

3. You can sneak in as much TV-watching as possible at your friends' houses.

It's tough when parents forbid TV in the home. But the worst that can happen is that you'll be:

- closer to your family

- more fit, less fat, and healthier

- better read and more successful in school

- a fascinating, creative, self-sufficient person with a million goals—and the intelligence and motivation to reach them

In the Kitchen

Kitchens are a prime source of calories, carbs, cholesterol, and conflict, as in:

> "Don't drink out of the milk carton."
> "Don't stand there with the refrigerator door hanging open."
> "Wipe up your crumbs."
> "Why is there a stack of dirty dishes in the sink?"
> "Who do you think I am, the maid?"

Following are the basics of proper kitchen behavior.

CLEAN UP AFTER YOURSELF. This means putting away food, sweeping up crumbs, wiping the counter, and rinsing off your dishes (or putting them in the dishwasher).

REPORT A SHORTAGE. If you eat the last piece of bread, drink the last gulp of milk, or scarf the last pineapple popsicle, tell someone—usually the person who does the food shopping for your household. Many families keep a shopping list on the refrigerator for this purpose. (There's no rule against trying to sneak your favorite foods onto the list.)

CHECK BEFORE YOU CHOMP. If something looks rare, special, and tempting, chances are it's not for you. It may be appetizers for company, or a cake for a bake sale. Ask.

PRETEND YOU'RE A WAITER. Let's say your family is watching TV together. If you get up to go to the kitchen for a soda or a sandwich, ask, "Can I get anybody anything?" It's rude to help yourself to food without offering some to others.

Of course, some people might abuse your courtesy. Family members may grow to count on your treks to the kitchen and stop getting up themselves. It's not fair if every time you say, "May I bring anyone anything from the kitchen?" you hear:

Dad: *"I'd love a ginger ale."*

Mom: *"A cup of tea would be nice."*

 Sister: *"Could you get me a grapefruit with the sections cut out? And a glass of water? And a napkin? And a spoon?"*

Brother: *"Yeah, bring me a ham-and-Swiss on whole wheat toast with lettuce, tomatoes, and mustard, tortilla chips with medium salsa, lemonade, juice, and three pickles. Don't let the pickle juice get on the bread."*

One hopes that with your good example, other members of your family will offer to make their fair share of runs to the kitchen. If they don't, you can always suggest that a different person be "on duty" each evening.

At the Table

For most teens, a family dinner is not a formal occasion. You don't have to worry about which fork to use and whether it's okay to ask for seconds. Still, there are some rules of behavior that make these meals more pleasant for everyone.*

COME WHEN CALLED. Wise parents will issue five-minute, three-minute, and "You'd-better-get-down-here-right-now-or-else" warnings.

PRESENT YOURSELF AT THE TABLE CLEAN AND CLOTHED. Face washed, hands washed, pants zipped, shirts on and buttoned, but *hats off.*

WAIT UNTIL EVERYONE SITS DOWN BEFORE STARTING TO EAT. Do this unless your mom or dad insists that you go ahead. ("I'll join you in a few minutes, after I put the chocolate soufflé in the oven. There's no need to let your mushroom bisque get cold.")

---

* Please note that we're talking about *dinner* here. Obviously, these rules won't work for breakfast. That's because family members arrive and depart at different times, depending on whether they're heading off to work, school, or wherever. Also, breakfast is the only meal where it's okay to read, wear your jammies, and sit in dazed silence, though it's polite to mumble "g'morning" when people arrive and "have a g'day" when they leave.

USE GOOD TABLE MANNERS. Here are the basics:

- Unfold your napkin and put it on your lap as soon as you sit down. Never tuck it under your chin. That's what bibs are for.

- Take small portions when food is passed.

- Sit up straight and lean slightly over the table when putting fork to mouth.

- Finish swallowing one mouthful before taking another (or a sip of your beverage).

- When eating, don't slurp. When drinking, don't gulp.

- Take small bites and chew with your mouth closed.

- Don't talk with your mouth full. What if someone asks you a question when you've just taken a bite of something? If the required answer is a simple yes or no, you can nod or shake your head. If a more detailed response is needed, give the "Wait-just-a-second-please" signal. You do this by raising your hand with your index finger up, as if you're testing for wind. If you want, you can also raise your eyebrows.

- Don't burp, belch, or pass gas at the table. If a sneaky little burp slips out, say, "Excuse me!" If you feel a belch or other gaseous act approaching, say, "Excuse me—I'll be right back," and make a quick exit. Get as far away from the table as you can.

- Keep your elbows off the table. You may, however, rest the undersides of your forearms on the table between bites or courses.

- Try to pace your eating so you don't get too far ahead of or behind everyone else.

- Don't play with your food.

- Don't push food around on your plate. There's one exception to this rule: If you're served something you don't like, move it around so it looks like it's getting some attention. Try to reduce its overall surface area. Meanwhile, make fascinating conversation. Then people will look at your brow, not your chow.

7 Reasonable Rules for Happy Home Dining

Should kids be forced to eat things they don't like? Generally, no. It's rude to cause others to gag, vomit, and keel over at the table. On the other hand, parents shouldn't have to cook five different meals every night to please picky family members. Follow these guidelines to find a middle ground:

1. Kids will try a bite of a new food before they can proclaim that they don't like it.

2. Parents will respect the right of underage taste buds to declare certain foods off-limits. Some kids simply will not eat breaded and fried squid bits (also known as calamari).

3. Kids who reject certain foods will not expect parents to prepare alternate meals for them.

4. Parents will make good-faith efforts to prepare meals that all family members like.

5. Kids will recognize that microwaved burritos are not nature's only food group and will try to eat a well-balanced diet.

6. Parents will recognize that kids can go quite a few days without vegetables or fruit before they begin to waste away.

7. Kids and parents together will determine policies to address the following questions:

   - Can a kid who doesn't like something make something else?

   - Can a kid who doesn't finish his dinner still have dessert?

   - Who decides portion size?

   - Can a kid who doesn't eat her dinner fix something later?

   - Can a kid snack between meals if it spoils his appetite?

▨ If you want something, don't reach across someone to get it. Ask, "Could you please pass the liver?" Platters should be passed from left to right (counterclockwise) around the table. That's because most people are right-handed, and it's easier to serve yourself by reaching across your plate to a dish on your left.

▨ If someone asks for the salt, pass the pepper, too. They get lonely without each other.

▨ If you drop food on the floor and you don't have a dog, retrieve it. If the food is pick-uppable (like a string bean or an apple slice), simply bend down, pick it up, and place it on the edge of your plate. If it's messier (like creamed corn or chili), excuse yourself, go get a spoon, sponge, or paper towel, and clean it up. If you drop a utensil, pick it up, excuse yourself, and get a clean one.

▨ If you must sop up that last bit of sauce, don't take a whole piece of bread and smear it across your plate. Instead, break off a small piece of bread, place it on your plate, spear it with your fork, and pretend it's a mop.

▨ Sometimes, what goes in must come out. A juicy piece of steak turns into a glob of gristle. An olive contains a pit. A tasty bite of fish hides a zillion bones. When this happens, be discreet. If it went in by fork, put it back on the fork and deposit it on your plate. An olive pit can go from your mouth to your hand to your plate. If you try to remove fish bones with a fork, you'll stab yourself in the face. Use your fingers.

Whenever I do something wrong at the table, my mother says, "Where were you brought up, in a barn?" It's so annoying! What can I say back?

"Moo." ◆

CONTRIBUTE TO THE CONVERSATION. Don't just sit there like a lump. Talk about current events, your day, future plans, whatever. Listen (or look like you're listening) when others talk.

STAY AT THE TABLE UNTIL PERMISSION IS GRANTED TO LEAVE. A parent might signal this moment by asking, "Whose turn is it to do the dishes?" If you must leave the table during the meal or before it's over, ask, "May I please be excused?" (**TIP:** Kids who say "May I?" instead of "Can I?" get bonus points.)

PARTICIPATE CHEERFULLY IN AFTER-DINNER CLEAN-UP CHORES. Do this if it's required. Do this if it's expected. Do it no matter what. At the very least, clear your own dishes from the table and put them in the sink or dishwasher.

SPOTLIGHT ON...
SHIRTLESSNESS

Home is where we should be most comfortable. For some young men, this means going shirtless. Especially on hot days, and even at the table.

This has been known to drive moms crazy. They believe that young men should wear shirts around the house at all times. Especially at the table, and even when mowing the lawn!

In general, when conflicts involve public areas, the "higher" standard of behavior (neatness, cleanliness, modesty) wins. But the "loser" retains the right to indulge himself in private. In other words: Whatever you wear (or don't wear) in your bedroom is fine. If your mother will agree to knock before entering, this will give you time to throw on a T-shirt (or whatever).

In the Bathroom

Bathrooms rank way up there on the list of family squabble generators:

"Mom, Christine's hogging the bathroom!"

"Who used up all the hot water?"

"Someone stole my shampoo!"

"Whose slimy hairball is that in the drain?!?"

"How many times have I told you, DON'T LEAVE WET TOWELS ON THE FLOOR!"
"Can't ANYONE remember to put the toilet seat down?"

Want to avoid these conflicts? All you have to do is install a 3,000-gallon water heater and hire a personal bathroom attendant for each family member.

Or you can establish a Fair Use Policy.

If six people all need to use the same bathroom within the space of 20 minutes, family members will stack up like planes at LaGuardia Airport in New York City. When needs conflict, try not to fight. Instead, work to solve the problem. Sit down with your family at a calm moment. Explain what you think the problem is, without blaming or accusing. ***Example:*** "The water is always cold when I take my shower," not "Jeffrey uses up all the hot water!" Then brainstorm solutions.

Maybe some people can shift to evening showers. Or get up earlier. Or use the laundry sink for shaving.

The solution may not be perfect, but it will be a lot better than starting every day with an argument.

 **Does it really matter how you squeeze the toothpaste tube? Our family gets into huge fights about this.**

It matters if your mom or dad thinks it matters. Train yourself to squeeze and roll from the bottom up. Or buy your own tube, squeeze it any way you like, and keep it out of sight. Or suggest that your family switch to toothpaste in a pump. No-squeeze is bound to pleeze. ◆

14 COMMANDMENTS
OF TOILETIQUETTE

THOU SHALT...

1. hang your towel on the rack

2. raise or lower the toilet seat, as the case may be (either way, make sure the seat is down and the lid is closed when you leave the bathroom)

3. willingly give way to those whose need is greater than yours

4. rinse out the tub after using it

5. remove your hairs from the soap and sink

6. clean the mirror after brushing and flossing

7. flush when you are done

THOU SHALT NOT...

8. pee on the toilet seat

9. finish a roll of toilet paper without replacing it

10. use more than your fair share of hot water

11. use the towels or other bathroom articles (razor, hair brush, lotion, shampoo) of others without their permission

12. enter without knocking and being invited in

13. comment on the sounds or scents generated by others

14. hang your drying socks or undies where they will hit others in the face

On the Phone

Some families these days have more than one phone line. So it's not as common as it once was to hear:

> "Mo-o-o-m! Make Dexter get off the phone! I'm waiting for a call and it's IMPORTANT!"
>
> "You've been on the phone for HOURS!"
>
> "Is the phone growing out of your EAR?!?"
>
> "GET OFF THE PHONE!!!!"

You may even have your own phone, or your own cell phone.

But there's probably still a family phone that everyone uses from time to time. When it rings, it's not always for you. Here's the well-mannered way to take a call:

SAY "HELLO." A cheerful "Hello" is all you need when answering a residential phone. It's not necessary to say "Pedigree residence, Bartholomew speaking," or, "Murray's Mortuary, you stab 'em, we slab 'em."

Your parents may want you to answer the phone in a particular way. If so, do as they ask.

DON'T SCREEN OTHER PEOPLE'S CALLS. If the call isn't for you, it's none of your business who's calling, no matter how curious you are. Don't inquire about the caller's identity unless your parents or siblings specifically ask you to. In that case, say to the caller, "May I tell them who's calling?"

DON'T YELL. It bugs parents no end when their kids answer the phone and scream, "MA! TELEPHONE! IT'S THAT LADY!" Put the phone down (or carry it, if it's a portable) and walk to where the person is. Then say, "Ma, telephone. It's that lady."

NEVER GIVE OUT PERSONAL INFORMATION. For safety's sake, don't tell strangers whether your parents are home or not. Don't give out your address or credit card numbers. And whatever you do, don't say that your dad is in the bathroom. People are never "in the bathroom" to callers. They are "unable to come to the phone."

GIVE THE CALLER YOUR FULL ATTENTION. It's rude to talk to someone while watching TV, carrying on other conversations, or typing away at your computer keyboard. Stop what you're doing and focus on the call.

IF THE PERSON BEING CALLED ISN'T AROUND, TAKE A MESSAGE. Write down the caller's name, the time of the call, the caller's phone number, and any brief message the caller wants to leave. Then, when the person being called gets home, *give him or her the message.* Even the best message-takers sometimes forget that last part.

What about when you do the dialing? Here's how to be a courteous caller:

ASK PERMISSION TO USE THE PHONE. If you want to use the family phone, and especially if you plan to talk for a while, check first to see if it's okay. Is Dad expecting a call? Does Mom want to phone her sister?

IF SOMEONE ELSE ANSWERS THE PHONE, ASK POLITELY FOR YOUR PARTY—THE PERSON YOU WANT TO SPEAK TO. Say:

"May I please speak to Muffy?"

Don't say:

"Is Muffy there?"

I learned this the hard way when I telephoned a friend and his four-year-old son answered the phone. "Is your daddy there?" I asked. "Yes," the boy said. After five minutes went by, insight dawned. "Could you please get him?" I asked. "Okay," the boy replied.

It's not necessary to tell the person who answers the phone who you are. But if you know the person, it's nice to say:

> "Hi, Mrs. Earwax, this is Mortimer Snerdhopper. May I please speak to Engelbert?"

Your friends' parents will think you're the politest teen in the world.

IDENTIFY YOURSELF WHEN YOU REACH YOUR PARTY. This has probably happened to you: You answer the phone, someone starts talking, and you don't have the slightest idea who it is. Unless you're calling a soul mate who would recognize your voice in a hurricane at 500 yards, say who you are. It could save you both from embarrassment. You know:

> "Hi, Freda, I know it's probably mean to call and say this over the phone, but I just have to tell you that I've decided to ask someone else to the dance this weekend, even though you and I have been getting along great and I know you were really wishing that I would ask you, and I hope we can still be friends and all…. What? This is Fred…. Fred Bates…. I sit behind you in math class…. Yeah, I'm the one with the big ears."

DON'T CALL AT INCONVENIENT TIMES. Since households eat and go to bed at all sorts of different hours, find out from your friends when it's okay and not okay to call. Many families don't appreciate interruptions during dinner or at 2:00 in the morning. It never hurts to ask, "Is this a good time to talk?" or, "How late is it okay to call?"

IF A STRANGE VOICE ANSWERS THE PHONE, DON'T JUST HANG UP OR SAY, "WHO'S THIS?" Ask for the person you're trying to call. If it turns out that you reached a wrong number, apologize. You may want to verify the number with the person who answered. That way, you'll know whether the number itself is wrong or you just misdialed.

SPOTLIGHT ON...

WHEN MAIL ISN'T ADDRESSED TO YOU

No matter how curious you are, never open or peek at mail that isn't yours. This includes postcards (but not underwear catalogs).

It's also improper to notice who's gotten mail from whom. For example, you would never ask your sister, "What did your ex-boyfriend want?" This suggests you know something that's none of your beeswax.

10 COMMANDMENTS
OF PHONETIQUETTE

THOU SHALT NOT...

1. make or take calls during dinner
2. eat while talking on the phone
3. carry on conversations with people in the room while talking on the phone
4. make prank phone calls
5. screen other people's calls unless asked to do so
6. hog the phone
7. listen in on other people's conversations
8. interrupt someone who's on the phone, unless it's an emergency
9. neglect to give the messages you take
10. beep, whistle, and pretend to be a fax machine

At the Computer

The family that computes together disputes together. If your family shares a computer, here's how to achieve keyboard harmony in your household.

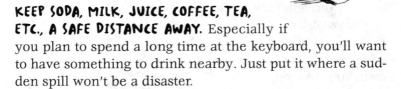

WASH YOUR HANDS BEFORE SITTING DOWN AT THE COMPUTER.
Nobody wants to see your lunch smeared all over the P, B, and J. Computing's no fun when QWERTY gets dirty.

KEEP SODA, MILK, JUICE, COFFEE, TEA, ETC., A SAFE DISTANCE AWAY. Especially if you plan to spend a long time at the keyboard, you'll want to have something to drink nearby. Just put it where a sudden spill won't be a disaster.

CLEAN HOUSE FREQUENTLY. Don't let your hard drive turn into a graveyard. Get rid of files that are ancient history and clutter up the machine for others.

BACK UP YOUR FILES. Just in case your little sister accidentally deletes your term paper, wouldn't you rather say, "Don't worry, I've got it on disc" than, "I'm going to KILL YOU!!!!"? In fact, make *two* sets of backup discs (or CD-ROMs) for important files. Keep one set at home. Keep the other set in your school locker or at a friend's home. This way, if there's ever a fire, burglary, or earthquake, or your house gets swallowed by a sinkhole, you'll still have a copy safe and sound.

Paranoid? Perhaps. But for the few seconds and few pennies this extra protection costs, isn't it worth it?

USE ANTIVIRUS SOFTWARE. If you're an active downloader, sooner or later your computer is going to get blasted with a virus. Be sure you protect the computer and everybody's files by using software that will guard you against viruses. Otherwise, your family is going to blast *you*.

DON'T TIE UP THE PHONE. If your connection is a dial-up and you spend hours each day surfing the Web or sending instant messages, this is bound to cause conflict with the rest of your family. With the phone tied up, they can't make or receive calls.

Before trouble brews, work out a fair use plan with your clan. Your best bet may be to install a separate phone line for the computer, or switch to cable. You can offer to split the cost or pay part. If there's competition for using the computer, you may need to work out a schedule so everyone gets the time they need.

RESPECT PEOPLE'S PRIVACY. Your computer may let users lock their files under a secret password. But that shouldn't be necessary. Snooping is R-U-D-E. Lead the way by promising never to look at anyone else's email or files.

A Few Choice Words About Swearing

It's not that swearing is "bad" in the sense that if you do it, you'll go to H-E-double-toothpicks. But there are three reasons why swearing is a bad idea:

1. **Too much swearing makes your mind go soggy.**
   People who swear all the time are boring to listen to:

   > "%*@&!-in'-A, man! I'm so %*@&!-in' mad. %*@&! him! I'm gonna %*@&! that %*@&!-er over, he won't know what the %*@&! hit him."

   A nine-word vocabulary doesn't allow for the expression of much insight, wit, intelligence, or empathy. If your speech is lazy, vague, and unimaginative, your mind is sure to follow.

2. **Too much swearing dilutes its shock value.** The whole purpose of swearing is to save a few words for special occasions. If you say "#@*%!" when you drop a sandwich, what do you say when an airplane drops a 300-pound block of frozen waste on your foot?

3. **Swearing is insensitive to the feelings of others.**
   Many people—maybe including your parents and

siblings—find swearing offensive. It wasn't that long ago that nobody ever swore. To swear in the presence of a lady was unthinkable. To swear around your mother was the worst. Children had their mouths washed out with soap for saying "damn." Some of us learned very young that Dial tastes better than Ivory Soap.

 **Every time I swear, my stepdad makes me give him ten cents. Do you think this is fair?**

Certainly not. He deserves at least a quarter. ◆

Fighting Fair

All families argue at times. In general, there's nothing wrong with arguing—as long as it's done with love and mutual respect. Arguing is okay if people listen to what others say, and work toward a resolution that respects everyone's needs and feelings. This is called *fighting fair*.

Unfair fighting is when people break or throw things, get violent toward each other, and/or say things they know will hurt. This kind of fighting rarely leads to resolving a conflict. It only makes it worse.

All families (especially large ones, where it's easy for individual voices to be lost) should have a family meeting once a week. This is a regularly scheduled time when everybody gathers to share news, set goals, air differences, and solve problems.

If your family already has family meetings, good for you. Read on to learn some ways to make them even better. If your family doesn't have family meetings, ask if they're willing to try.

How to Make Family Meetings Work

SET A REGULAR TIME TO MEET. If someone can't come, try to reschedule. If someone just decides not to show up, don't reschedule. It's their loss, and they have to live with decisions made without their input.

PUT AN AGENDA WHERE EVERYONE CAN SEE IT. Stick it on the fridge with a magnet, or leave it on the kitchen counter. Family members can use it to write down items they'd like to discuss at the meeting. Late-breaking issues can always be brought up, but advance planning helps the meeting go smoother.

APPOINT A "CHAIR" FOR EACH MEETING. This is the person who brings the agenda and runs the meeting. The position should be rotated among family members so no one person is in charge every time.

DON'T MEET FOR TOO LONG. When people get restless, tempers flare up and thinking gets sloppy. Better to schedule another meeting than to run overtime.

TAKE NOTES. Appoint a scribe for each meeting. The scribe's job is to write down ideas, decisions, plans, etc. He or she can also remind people between meetings of actions they need to take.

SOLVE PROBLEMS WITH STRUCTURED PROBLEM-SOLVING. See pages 46–47.

KEEP THE MOOD POSITIVE. While family meetings are the place to bring problems and complaints, they shouldn't turn into gripe sessions. This can be avoided if you all agree to the following rules:

- Listen when others speak.

- Focus on solving problems, not winning arguments.

- Don't label other people's ideas "dumb" or "clueless."

- Say how you feel without blaming or accusing.

- Include at least one fun item on every agenda. *Examples:* making vacation plans; deciding what to do for Grandma's birthday.

- End each meeting on an upbeat note. Rent a video, make ice cream sundaes, or play a game. Try not to end a meeting when people are angry or upset.

How to Solve Family Problems

Often, family problems lead to arguments, fights, and hard feelings that last for days, weeks, even years. That's one reason there are so many therapists in the world. In fact, many family problems can be solved using a five-step process called Structured Problem-Solving.

1. **Define the problem without blaming or accusing.** Talk about your needs and feelings, not why or how the other person is making your life miserable. *Example:* "I can't study when music is playing," not "Henry's music is driving me crazy!!!"

2. **Brainstorm solutions together.** Come up with as many ideas as you can. The more the merrier; the sillier the better. Sometimes it's the wild ideas that lead to the best solutions. At this stage, no criticism or commentary is allowed. The scribe writes down any and all ideas. *Examples:* Henry could wear headphones. You could wear earplugs. All music-playing could be banned during homework hours.

3. **Discuss the ideas you came up with.** Which ones seem impractical? Unrealistic? Don't say, "That's stupid!" Say, "I don't think that would work because...." *Example:* "I don't think wearing ear plugs would work because I couldn't hear Fluffy bark when she needs to go out." "I don't think banning music would work because Janet couldn't practice her violin." For solutions you think would work, say, "I like that idea because...."

4. **Choose one to try, and decide how to carry it out.**
Which one seems most likely to solve the problem?
Example: Henry could wear headphones. He can
borrow yours while he saves up money to buy his own.

5. **Track your progress.** How are things going? Is the
solution working out? Why or why not? If it is, congrat-
ulate each other. If it isn't, try something else.

SPOTLIGHT ON...
WHEN YOUR PARENTS DOCK YOUR ALLOWANCE

Sometimes, when kids do things parents don't like, parents respond by withholding or stopping their allowance.

Personally, I believe that kids should get an allowance with no strings attached. Because they're family members, they should get a small share of the family income. They shouldn't have to beg their mom or dad for money every time they want to buy a CD or a pack of gum.

Before you run to your parents and show them this page, there's something else you should know: I also believe that kids should do more around the house than collect an allowance. Because they're family members, they should act like it. This means doing chores and meeting certain standards of behavior. You're not keeping your part of the bargain if you forget or refuse to do your chores, if you're rude, if you won't cooperate, and if you're a pain in the butt.

When your parents dock your allowance, here are two things you can try:

1. Stop the behaviors your parents don't like.

2. Suggest other consequences for your actions.
   Example: You won't go out with your friends until you do your chores.

Now you can run to your parents and show them this page.

How to Apologize

Many family problems can be solved with two little words: "I'm sorry." Yet, for some people, they're as hard to say as the three little words "I love you." And often, people say them without meaning them.

Sometimes, when kids are embarrassed, angry, or defensive, they mutter a quick "Sorry!" Even if they really are sorry, this doesn't get communicated. Instead, parents hear, "Why are you making such a big deal about this?"

An even worse form of apology is, "Well, I *said* I'm sorry!" This comes across as "Get off my back!"

If you want your apologies to be accepted, show that you're sorry in word and deed. Saying you're sorry is only half an apology. Doing something about it is the other half.

The next time your mom scolds you for something you did wrong, try saying something like this:

"Oh, no, I can't believe I did such a thing. I'm such a mush mind. I'll never be able to look myself in the mirror again. You must think I'm the worst child that ever lived. I wouldn't blame you if you grounded me for life. I promise I'll be much more careful in the future."

Then offer to set things straight. Your mom may take you up on your offer. Or she may be so impressed by the sincerity of your words that she'll be satisfied.

Sharing a Room

In the adult world, you generally get to choose your room-mates. And if things don't work out, you can unchoose.

With kids, it's different. You're forced to share a room with your sister or brother—or maybe several sisters or brothers. If you're lucky, this can lead to closeness, good times, and great memories. If you're unlucky, it can ruin your life.

Meanwhile, parents aren't very sympathetic. They tell you that sharing a room is a "learning experience." And that "you need to learn how to live with people you don't always get along with." You say, "Isn't that what marriage is for?" But it doesn't do any good. You're stuck.

Sibling Survivalry

Siblings can be a joy to live with—IF you know the secrets of proper roommate etiquette. The key to getting along with roommates is to lock them in the closet until they behave. If that's not an option, try *consideration* and *negotiation.*

CONSIDERATION means thinking about the consequences of your actions—how they might affect others. It's not enough to imagine what might happen if you do something, then do it anyway. ("Hmmm, if I threw a water balloon, he'd probably get wet. Ready...set...THROW!") You want to imagine what might happen, then *not do* something that could infringe on the rights, property, and serenity of others.

If you're not sure, you can always ask:

"Is it okay if I throw this water balloon at you?"

"Do you mind if I get rid of this, or are you doing a science project about three-month-old bologna sandwiches?"

"Is it all right with you if I rearrange the furniture and put your bed in the basement?"

NEGOTIATION helps when roommates have conflicting wants, needs, tastes, and metabolisms. ***Examples:*** You need to throw a water balloon; your roommate needs to stay dry. You prefer to see the floor; your roommate prefers to hang her clothes on it. You like to be warm at night; your roommate wants the window open, even when it's 40 degrees below zero.

This doesn't mean that all siblings who share space are destined to fight. Your roommate may be as kind, polite, thoughtful, generous, and cool as you are. If that's the case, just skip the rest of this chapter.

If it's not, read on.

(pause)

I thought so.

Resolving Roommate Problems

Conflict is natural and sometimes even healthy. Conflict is not what harms relationships. It's *unresolved* or *unfairly resolved* conflict that does the damage.

While kindness, consideration, and empathy go a long way toward preventing problems, some conflict will happen. Try to recognize it early and address it in ways that respect people's needs and feelings.

People who share space are bound to have conflicts because they have different ideas of noise and neatness, different tastes, different daily rhythms, different priorities and attitudes, and different lots of other things. To prevent problems from growing into giant-sized conflicts, try some Structured Problem-Solving.*

1. Define the problem without blaming or accusing.

2. Brainstorm solutions together.

---

* If you haven't yet read pages 46–47, there's an example of Structured Problem-Solving at work.

3. Discuss the ideas you came up with.

4. Choose one to try, and decide how to carry it out.

5. Track your progress.

This strategy can be applied to almost any conflict as long as your goal is *fairness,* not just *winning.* It assumes that the conflict is about a *difference,* not who's "right" or who's "wrong."

Sometimes it's hard to tell who's "right" and who's "wrong." That's when these guidelines come in handy for choosing what to do:

■ Legal behavior wins out over illegal behavior.

■ Rule-following behavior beats rule-breaking behavior. (Although, if both roommates agree to break the rules, this is no longer an issue of etiquette and they may do so at their own risk.)

■ Health comes first. ***Example:*** Allergies to animal hair outrank the desire to keep a pet llama in the room.

■ Virtuous behavior goes first before nonvirtuous behavior. Virtuous behavior is creative, productive, considerate, giving, and good. Nonvirtuous behavior is selfish, dishonest, mean, disgusting, and bad. But let's not get carried away. The virtuous roommate does not have the right to act stuck-up and superior.

What do you do when *both* roommates are "right"? Look for the easiest, most sensible solution. ***Examples:***

1. Your roommate wants to play music. You want to study. *Solution:* It's easier for your roommate to wear headphones than it is for you to leave the room.

2. You like to sleep with the window open (room temperature a nippy 50 degrees). Your roommate likes to sleep with it closed (room temperature a toasty 80 degrees). *Solution:* It's easier to get warm in a cool environment than it is to keep cool in a warm environment. Crack the window open a bit (room temperature 63 degrees) and lend your down comforter to your roommate.

As a last resort, roommates can petition the authorities for a divorce. Maybe you can swap with someone else who's unhappy with his or her living situation. Or scour the house for a corner that might be turned into a space for yourself.

SPOTLIGHT ON...

NEATNESS
VS. MESSINESS

What if your roommate is a neatnik and you're a slobnik? Then you've got a conflictnik. Dust off the problem-solving strategy outlined on pages 53–54. Brainstorm solutions—like these:

- Hang blankets or build a partition to divide the space. (This way, you won't have to look at the neatness.)

- Define okay and not-okay messes. *Examples:* Cluttered desk—okay. Food on floor—not okay.

- Schedule a time once a week when you turn up the music and blitz the room with a thorough cleanup.

- Hire a sibling to clean for you.

- Get a trunk or a big box. Throw the things you used to throw on the floor in there instead.

Do you have your own room? Be as messy as you want, as long as you:

- Keep the door to your room shut.

- Follow your parents' rules for neatness in the rest of the house.

- Don't allow mutant life forms to grow on leftover food and overripe clothing.

- Don't violate housing or safety codes.

- Repair, replace, or do without things you break or lose in your pigsty, er, room.

Some parents might argue against letting kids be messy, but they should get a life. Neatness is a learned skill. It comes with age as children decide they don't want to spend half their days looking for things, or half their allowances replacing things they step on. It comes when a friend visits and says, "How can you live in this room, er, pigsty?"

Isn't making your bed a total waste of time?

Yes, because you're only going to unmake it again. And no, because of all those hours in between. A made-up bed looks neater than an unmade bed. This matters to some people, probably including your parents and maybe your roommate if you share a room.

But bed-making shouldn't be a big hairy deal. Aim for speed and efficiency. Avoid thin bedspreads with busy plaid patterns—they take too long to line up and straighten out. Get a thick, fluffy comforter or quilt instead. You can fling it over your bed in three seconds. If the sheets are bunched up underneath, who cares? ◆

5 COMMANDMENTS
OF ROOMIE-ETIQUETTE

It's very important for roommates to respect each other's privacy because there isn't any. Since *physical* privacy is usually impossible to achieve, you have to create *psychological* privacy. Therefore:

THOU SHALT NOT...

1. read your roommate's letters, email, journals, or papers

2. snoop through your roommate's desk and dresser drawers

3. borrow your roommate's possessions without asking

4. reveal personal things you learn from living with your roommate ("Hey, guys, guess what! My brother James drools in his sleep!")

5. rat on your roommate, unless his or her actions put you or anyone else in danger

Having Friends Over

It's fun to go out with friends—to movies, dances, the go-kart track. It's great to hang out with friends—at the mall, the park, the coffee shop. But it's even better to bring friends home, where the living is easy and the snacks are free.

Unless you made millions as a child actor and can now afford to live on your own, it's not just *your* home. Other people live there, too. As a host, you're responsible for making your guests feel welcome. As a family member, it's best to keep some basic manners in mind. You also need to see that your guests use good behavior—especially if they want to be invited back.

The 10 Rudest Things Teens' Friends Do When They Visit

• •

When we asked adults, "What are the rudest things your children's friends do in your home?" these were the top 10 answers:

1. Come in without saying "Hello" and/or leave without saying "Good-bye."

2. Not say "Please" or "Thank you."

3. Throw their shoes, jackets, and backpacks all over.

4. Are loud and disrespectful.

5. Not thank parents for fixing snacks, picking them up, etc.

6. Damage or break things without apologizing or offering to replace them.

7. Hint for things they can't have, or ask for them outright.

8. Not look parents in the eye.

9. Not talk to them.

10. Wander into every room without asking.

Parents also complained about friends who raid the refrigerator, use bad language, look in cabinets and drawers, flip through mail, question house rules, and turn on the TV or use the computer without asking permission first.

Hosting the After-School Guest

This is hosting at its most informal. Strays brought home from school may enter and exit so quickly that their presence goes unnoticed—except for the unwashed dishes on the kitchen counter. Sometimes after-school visitors travel in packs, roaming from place to place in search of the perfect snack.

In time, these frequent fliers may come in for so many landings at your home that their status changes from guest to semi-family member. This brings special rights and responsibilities. Rights include greater access to your family's trust, affection, and refrigerator. Your parents will relax and be themselves. Your friends will get to hear real family squabbles and see your mother without makeup.

But all this comes at a cost. Honorary family members lose special guest status. Like their "siblings," they are expected to help with kitchen clean-up, trash duty, table-setting, and more.

Here are your responsibilities as a host for after-school guests:

COMMUNICATE WITH YOUR PARENTS. Is it okay to bring friends home from school without asking? What if your parents aren't there? Can you invite friends to stay for a meal? Avoid misunderstandings by negotiating and knowing your parents' expectations ahead of time.

INTRODUCE YOUR FRIENDS TO YOUR FAMILY. In general, parents like to know the names of those who are eating their food, watching their television, sprawling on their furniture, and leaving their smelly shoes by the door. You can keep introductions simple:

> "Mom, this is Ken Tuckey. He's just moved here from Topeka. And you already know Biff, Bill, Bob, Ben, Bart, Brett—and Sticky."

EXPLAIN HOUSE RULES. You're not bossing your guests around. You're helping them avoid embarrassment and worse. You can word the rules so they sound like concerns for your guests' comfort and safety:

> "It's best if you don't go into my sister's room. She can be a terror, and I can't guarantee you'd get out of there alive."

> "Hey, could you please not stand on the coffee table? I'd feel awful if it broke and you got glass up your nose."

You can also state house rules as coming straight from your parents. They're not *your* rules, but you're required to enforce them:

> "I'm afraid my dad doesn't let us play croquet with the crystal."
>
> "Sorry, but my stepmom doesn't allow wrestling in the house."
>
> "My folks get very upset when people paint the dog."

HELP WITH EXTRA BURDENS. Your parents may truly enjoy your friends and not mind that their house doubles as a community recreation center. Still, running a home for wayward teens involves extra work and expense. Do what you can to lessen the load. After you've finished eating, put away the food (if there's any left). Stack plates, glasses, and silverware in the dishwasher. Straighten the furniture. Your parents may not complain about the extra 73 gallons of milk, 144 loaves of bread, and 35 quarts of peanut butter your friends consume each week if you do your part.

KEEP YOUR GUESTS BUSY. Few things annoy parents more than bored kids hanging around the house. If being bored is one of your favorite things, do it where your parents can't see you. Otherwise, you're going to hear, "If you guys have nothing to do, the garage needs cleaning." Suggest to your friends that you shoot some hoops, surf the Web, watch a video, play a game, redecorate your bedroom, etc.

DON'T USE GUESTS TO GET AWAY WITH MURDER. Some teenagers wait for guests to come over to break house rules. They're betting on the fact that their parents won't scold them in front of their guests. This is unwise for two reasons. First, it only delays the scolding. Second, it takes unfair advantage of parents who respect their kids' feelings enough to not embarrass them in front of their friends. You should be on your *best* behavior when guests are around, not your worst. This clears the way for more guests in the future.

Hosting Groups

Your first responsibility is to issue a clear invitation. Maybe some friends who have been to your house 17,892 times know that "Ya wanna come over Friday?" means "Do you want to take the bus home from school with me, stay for dinner, go to a movie, spend the night, and sleep until 1:00 P.M. the next day?" Other friends who don't know you as well might be confused by what "come over" means.

Before your guests arrive, they should know what they're arriving for. Otherwise they'll worry about what to wear, what to bring, how to pack, and when to tell their parents to pick them up.

Every invitation, written or verbal, should contain the following information:

- *The Event:* Is it a birthday party? A swim party? A Super Bowl party?

- *The Time:* When does it begin and end?

- *The Place:* Is it at your home? The skating rink? The park?

- *The Hosts:* Are you the only host? Or is another friend co-hosting?

- *The Attire:* Snowsuits? Bathing suits? Tuxedos?

- *The Response:* Just show up? Call if you can come? Call only if you can't come?

In addition, the invitation should contain any special instructions needed for the event's success and the guests' comfort, such as:

Please bring rope, shaving cream, and sleeping bags.
Sunblock and insect repellent recommended!
Don't forget to bring a bike helmet.

Here's how to make your guests feel welcome when they arrive:

ANSWER THE DOOR. Guests feel dumb if they ring the bell and nobody comes to the door. They don't know whether to ring again and risk feeling dumber, or to walk in and risk being mistaken for a burglar.

GREET YOUR GUESTS. Say, "Hello. It's great you could come." Every guest should be made to feel that now the party can begin.

TAKE COATS. Visitors often arrive with coats, bags, and, if you're lucky, gifts. Take them or tell guests where they can put them.

SAY "THANK YOU" IF YOU ARE HANDED A GIFT. But don't dump your guest to go open it. You wouldn't want to give the impression that you're more interested in her *presents* than her *presence*.

OFFER NOURISHMENT. Take beverage orders. ("What can I get you? Juice, soda, iced tea, lemonade?") Or, if the event is self-serve, point your guests toward the food and drink.

MAKE INTRODUCTIONS. Smooth your guests' entry. Introduce them to people they don't know. Provide conversation cues to get things started:

> "Beefy's been my trainer at the gym."
> "Chilly works with me at the Scoop-and-Slurp."
> "Roscoe raises Rottweilers. Ask him about his dogs."

CIRCULATE. Spend time with *all* of your guests. Don't focus on your closest friends and ignore everyone else.

SEE THAT EVERYONE HAS A GOOD TIME. Make sure that no one is excluded from group activities. On the other hand, make sure that no one feels pressured into group activities they want to avoid.

THANK YOUR GUESTS FOR COMING. When the party or event is over, tell your guests how much you enjoyed having them. Walk them to the door. Say you can't wait to see them again. They'll leave with a warm glow.

 **I get invited to a lot of parties, and I want to have one of my own. But my parents won't let me. Aren't you supposed to invite people who have invited you?**

Certainly. This is known as *reciprocation.* It's how we thank people for their hospitality. It also keeps invitations coming our way.

Parents who won't let their children entertain usually have their reasons. Some are practical, and some are silly. If you don't know your parents' reasons, ask them. Approach them when they're in a good mood. Ask like this:

"I'm curious about something. Could you please tell me your reasons for not wanting me to have a party?"

not like this:

"Why can't I have a party? That's sooooo unfair! Everyone else's parents let them have parties!!! You're meaaaaannnnnn!"

Once your parents have told you their reasons, thank them and drop the subject for now. Meanwhile, come up with a plan that addresses their concerns. Too expensive? You'll share the cost. House too small? You'll have your party at the rink. Fear of crashers? You'll ask your friends from the football team to be bouncers. If it's still no go, maybe you could co-host a party at a friend's home.

You can also reciprocate in other ways. Buy or make a gift. Bake a pie. Your friends will know you appreciate their invitations, even if you're not able to return the favor. ◆

Petiquette

You're sitting on the sofa in your friend's TV room. The family dog comes up to you and nuzzles at your crotch. Do you:

(a) pretend it isn't happening?

(b) punch the dog and ask your friend, "What kind of a pervert animal is this?"

(c) steer the dog's snout away, allowing your friend to apologize and say, "Down, Snoop! Bad dog!"

Sooner or later, you're bound to be the target of a curious pet. When this happens, you have the right to just say no to the nose that goes *sniff sniff snurfffff* at your privates.

Of course, you wouldn't have this problem if other people exercised more control over the nonhuman members of their family. Call me unfriendly, but I have never developed a liking for creatures that leave muddy pawprints on my clothes or shake their smelly, flea-infested hair in my face.

I am all for animal rights, as long as animals keep their paws, snouts, and slobber to themselves. If they don't, it's the owner, not the animal, who's guilty of being rude.

So you don't join the ranks of impolite pet owners, here's all the petiquette you need to know:

CONTROL YOUR PET. Guests should not be assaulted or smothered with affection by any member of your household—unless they say it's okay:

> "I don't mind at all if Max the Mastiff puts his paws on my shoulders and licks my face."

> "It's no problem if Felix the Cat uses my leg for a scratching post."

> "It's perfectly fine with me if Bob the Boa crawls up my pant leg."

> "Sure, Tommy Tarantula can sit in my lap. I love big, hairy spiders!"

RESPECT YOUR GUESTS' SENSITIVITIES AND/OR PHOBIAS. Some people are allergic to feathers and pet hair. Others are simply terrified of animals. If you discover that either is true for one of your guests (because he's covered in hives, or she's hiding in a closet), do something about it. No, don't laugh, point, and call the person a wuss. Remove the animal from the room and put it somewhere else—in another room, in the backyard, in its crate or cage or tank.

If you refuse to restrict your animals' freedom, you must let guests know this in advance. You can say:

> "I can't wait 'til Friday, when you're all coming over after school. I just wanted to let you know that I have a verrrrrry friendly ferret. I'm sure you'll get on famously, but...."

Most people will tell you how much they're looking forward to meeting your family—two-footed, four-footed, hairy or not. If, however, one of your friends says, "Ferret? I don't like ferrets. Ever since one tried to chew my face off when

I was five...," you have only two choices: Uninvite your friend, or keep the ferret in a secure area until your friend leaves.

TAKE RESPONSIBILITY FOR YOUR PET'S BEHAVIOR. If your pet bites someone, soils her clothes, or damages her property, it's fair and proper for you to assume the medical, cleaning, or repair costs. (Whether you take it out of your dog's allowance later is for you to decide.) At the time of the incident, there's only one thing to do: Apologize profusely and make things right. Don't try to shift or minimize your responsibility.

WRONG	RIGHT
"It didn't even break the skin."	"We must get a doctor to look at that right away."
"I'm sure it will brush right off when it dries."	"I insist on having it dry cleaned for you."
"You should watch where you step."	"Oh, dear. I guess he's not totally housebroken after all. You can borrow a pair of my sneakers while I try to clean that off."
"Dogs will be dogs."	"I should have told you that Fifi likes to chew on backpacks. How much do I owe you?"

If you've got a reputation as a caring, responsible pet owner, the victims of your pet's misconduct will probably say something like:

"It's just a little bruise."

"It's only a small slobber. No big deal."

"Those shoes were too small for me anyway."

"Never mind. It was an old backpack."

You can then give in to their wishes. But you will have fulfilled your duties as a polite pet owner.

What about when you're invited to someone else's home? Follow this simple rule:

NEVER BRING A PET WITH YOU UNLESS YOU HAVE RECEIVED PERMISSION. You would never bring an uninvited friend to a party without first asking the host. (At least, I hope you wouldn't.) Similarly, you should never bring an uninvited animal. Clear the way, make sure it's okay, and you'll get invited back another day—with or without your potbellied pig.

What if you're not a pet owner, but someone who comes into contact with other people's pets? Then you're a *pettee*. Here's the petiquette that pertains to you:

BE KIND TO ANIMALS. It's rude to cut worms in half or throw cats from a moving train. Animals are living creatures. For that reason alone, they deserve respect. Don't tease or torture them.

ASK THE PET'S OWNER FOR GUIDANCE. With some animals you meet, it will be love at first sight. A bond will form instantly. This is called *animal magnetism*. You'll know without words that it's fine for the two of you to nuzzle and snuzzle all over the ground in an ecstasy of furry friendship. At other times, you and the animal may be unsure of each other. In such cases, ask the owner if it's all right to pat the dog, feed the horse, stroke the bird, or tap the turtle. **TIP:** You should never pet or call to a service animal such as a guide dog without the owner's permission. This could distract the animal and/or interfere with its training.

BE FIRM BUT POLITE ABOUT YOUR LIMITS. Animals seem to know instinctively who likes them and who doesn't. In a room of 12 people, the Doberman will be drawn to the one person who can't stand dogs. He'll track that person down and ignore all others. If you happen to be that unlucky person, it's perfectly fine to protest. Start with the animal. Remove its head or body from wherever it is you don't

want it to be. In a firm but respectful voice, say, "Down!" or "No!" Many animals are sensitive to the language of rejection. If, however, the Dobe doesn't take the hint, turn to its master and say:

> "Rex, could you please keep Tex away from me? He's a beauty for sure, but I'm just not comfortable around animals."

If your host doesn't control the beast, you might innocently remark:

> "Have you noticed the price of dry cleaning these days?"

Or:

> "I can't believe what they charge at the emergency room to treat an animal bite."

 **My neighbor's dog goes to the bathroom in our backyard. This is a real pain because my friends and I like to play baseball there. What can I do?**

This gives new meaning to the term "sliding into home."

You should start by providing the dog's owner with the scoop on the poop. Do this in a polite tone of voice. Suggest that you're sure he couldn't possibly know about the problem, since otherwise it wouldn't be happening. Ask him if he could please keep his dog in his own yard from now on.

If this doesn't work, there's just one thing left to do: The right thing. The polite thing. The thing that's sure to get your neighbor's attention. Can you guess? Here's a hint: It's courteous to return things that guests have left at your house by mistake.

So go out on your own (or with your friends), collect a sacka caca from your yard, and put it in your neighbor's yard—maybe even near his front door. No, don't light it on fire. Never play with matches! Instead, you might attach a brief note. Don't sign it with your real name. A gift this generous should remain anonymous. ◆

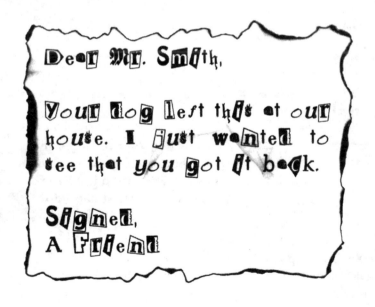

Dear Mr. Smith,

Your dog left this at our house. I just wanted to see that you got it back.

Signed,
A Friend

The Blended, Shaken, Stirred, or Extended Family

There are so many types of families these days that no single definition covers them all. A mom, dad, two kids, and a dog? Sometimes. A mom, dad, stepdad, stepmom, two siblings, four stepsiblings, a dog, and a stepdog? Two moms, four kids, and a foster kid? A dad, a grandmother, six cousins, and a hundred hamsters?

These are all possibilities, along with lots of others. You might be born into a particular type of family, then watch it change before your eyes. The most common type of change these days is divorce.

Do's and Don'ts for Children of Divorce

When parents get divorced, it's not only your home life that's affected. Friends, neighbors, and acquaintances ask questions like:

"Why are your parents splitting up?"
"Who are you going to live with?"
"Whose fault was it?"

But it's none of their business, and you don't feel like talking about it. What's the polite way to respond? Just say:

"I prefer not to discuss these things, thank you."

Some of the kids (and adults) who ask you these questions are simply rude boors sniffing for juicy gossip. Others, however, are sincere and mean well. While their questions may be nosy and clumsy, what they're really saying is, "I'm here if you want to talk."

You have every right to keep your personal life private. But I hope you'll talk about your feelings with someone you trust—a parent, teacher, close friend, or relative. Teenagers whose parents are going through a breakup can feel scared, angry, ashamed, and guilty. They sometimes blame themselves for the divorce, or think their parents won't love them anymore, or decide it's up to them to get their parents back together. These feelings, if kept bottled up inside, can make it hard for kids to concentrate, enjoy life, trust people, and build new family relationships.

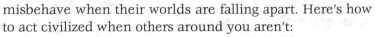

Talking about your feelings doesn't mean spilling the beans on private family matters. It means taking care of *you* at a time when your parents might not be doing such a great job. They may be too stunned, too sad, or too busy trashing each other.

Divorce can bring out the worst in everyone. Even well-mannered boys and girls have been known to misbehave when their worlds are falling apart. Here's how to act civilized when others around you aren't:

DO PUT YOURSELF IN YOUR PARENTS' SHOES. They, too, may feel angry, confused, scared, lonely, and betrayed. Try to help each other rather than hurt each other.

DON'T GET CAUGHT IN THE MIDDLE OF YOUR PARENTS' ARGUMENTS. As you leave the room, say, "I love you both, but I'm not going to take sides."

DON'T ASK ABOUT THE REASONS FOR THE BREAKUP. These are your parents' business, not yours. Try to respect their privacy.

DO ASK HOW THE DIVORCE WILL AFFECT YOUR LIFE. Where will you live? How often will you see the parent you don't live with? Will you have to move? Will you have to change schools? These are details you have the right to know.

DON'T PLAY ONE PARENT OFF AGAINST THE OTHER. *Example:* "Daddy doesn't mind if I stay out 'til two in the morning, so I don't know why you do."

DON'T CARRY MEAN OR ANGRY MESSAGES FROM ONE PARENT TO ANOTHER. *Examples:* "Tell your mother that she'll get her money when they pry it from my cold, dead fingers!" "Tell your father that I won't let you go to his house when SHE's there, and if he doesn't like that, he can take me to court!"

DO CARRY HELPFUL MESSAGES FROM ONE PARENT TO ANOTHER. *Examples:* "Tell your mom that I'll pick you up at eight." "Tell your dad that I'll be late to the school conference, but you all start without me." (**TIP:** If these get to be too much, you might say, "You know, I can barely remember everything I have to do in my own life. Would you mind calling mom and telling her yourself?")

**DON'T TELL YOUR PARENTS ABOUT EACH OTHER'S LIVES—
EVEN IF THEY WANT YOU TO.** How to handle this politely?
Like this:

> Parent: *"So, is your dad seeing anyone these days?"*
> Teen: *"You'll have to ask him about that, Mom."*

> Parent: *"So, did your mom get that raise she was hoping for?"*
> Teen: *"You'll have to ask her about that, Dad."*

DO BE POLITE TO YOUR PARENTS' NEW ROMANTIC INTERESTS.
Treat them with the same courtesy you extend toward all
guests.

**DON'T ASSUME THAT YOUR PARENTS' DATES WISH TO STEAL
YOUR MOM OR DAD'S AFFECTIONS FROM YOU.** It's a different
kind of affection they're after.

**DON'T ASK YOUR PARENTS FOR DETAILS OF WHAT THEY DO
ON OR WITH DATES.** You really don't want to know.

**DON'T BRAG ABOUT ONE PARENT'S "NEW FRIEND" TO THE
OTHER PARENT.** *Example:* "He's so cool, Dad. He drives a
Corvette and he said he'd teach me to fly his helicopter!"

DO GIVE STEPPARENTS A BREAK. It's as hard for them as it is
for you.

SPOTLIGHT ON...
NAME-CALLING

Let's pretend that you have a stepfather. You call him "Larry" because his name is Larry Barry. But what should your friends call him?

Whatever he asks them to. If he doesn't ask for anything specific, they should call him "Mr. Barry." And if they don't know his last name, they should call him "Sir" until they learn what it is. Which should be your cue to make proper introductions all around. *Example:* "Larry, these are my friends Gary and Harry. Gary and Harry, this is my stepdad, Mr. Barry."

Now, what about adoptive vs. biological parents, half-brothers vs. full brothers, and the parents of your father's second wife? How on earth do you introduce them?

Keep in mind that introductions are a kind of social short-hand. They are designed to give a general idea of people's roles and functions. There's no need to hand out DNA samples or genealogical charts. And there's no need to correct people who make the wrong assumption, unless that causes harm or embarrassment. *Examples:*

- People are always telling you that you look like your mother. In fact, she's not your biological mother. Should you say, "Oh, that's just a coincidence. Even though she's raised me for the past ten years, she's not my birth mother, who ran away and joined the circus when I was in first grade"? No. A simple "Thanks!" is enough.

- The conductor of your school orchestra says, "I really enjoyed meeting your parents at the concert." Should you say, "Oh, that wasn't my father. That was my mother's boyfriend who lives with us"? Probably not. Again, "Thanks!" will do. But what if your father is coming to the next concert? You might want to say, "Actually, that was a friend of my mother's. My father will be attending next week. I hope you can meet him."

As long as everyone's comfortable, it's perfectly okay to call your half-brothers "brothers," your stepmother "Mom," and the parents of your father's second wife "Grandma" and "Grandpa."

If you're really stuck, you can introduce someone as a "family friend," "one of my relatives," or simply by their name. That's a lot better than saying, "I'd like you to meet the fiancée of my once-the-divorce-is-final ex-stepmother's soon-to-be husband's sister-in-law's son."

Relating to Relatives

We can choose our friends, but not our families. And especially not our extended families. This is a shame, because they seem to include a lot of people who bore us to death, ask prying questions, and annoy us in other ways.

You might be tempted to avoid your relations. This would be a mistake. It's very important to see them and stay in touch with them. Why? Because this gives you the chance to get in good with rich aunts, lord it over the less fortunate branches of the family tree, and keep family feuds alive.

Also, family is a precious thing. When push comes to shove, when you're down on your luck, who else will you turn to for love, support, and loans?

So don't think of visits to rela-  tives as dreary chores. Think of them as opportunities. Change your *attitude* and you'll change your *experience*.

Instead of being passive, be active. What about the visit bothers you the most? The food? Sitting around indoors talking? Doing the same things every time you visit? No other kids around? The fact that the TV is constantly blaring and it's always on Fox news or a shopping channel? No matter what it is, you can do something about it.

- Volunteer to help with the cooking.

- Bring a board game and ask if people want to play it with you.

- Suggest that you all take a walk around the neighborhood or to the nearest interesting place: a park, a hiking path, a museum, the shore.

- Explore the neighborhood on your own. Bring your bike if you have one, or borrow a relative's bike. Or go on foot. If you see any kids, stop and talk to them.

- With your relatives' permission, invite a friend along. (You may have to promise that you'll go with her to *her* relatives' at some future date.)

▦ Instead of sitting there being bored, try talking about things that interest you. (**TIP:** This is a *great* opportunity to find out more about your parents. Go off with your aunts and uncles and grandparents and ask them for the scoop on your folks as kids.)

▦ What are your relatives into? Maybe one of them knows a lot about music, or photography, or knitting, or paper airplanes. Use the visit as a chance to learn new skills and knowledge.

▦ Bring one of *your* interests into the visit. Play your guitar. Take some family pictures, then make mini-albums to bring next time. Show off your latest art project or magic trick. Whatever.

About that blaring TV: It's rude to leave the TV on when company comes.* It's also rude to insist that people turn off their TV when you're a guest in their home. Here are two gentler tactics you can try:

1. **Speak extra-softly.** When your relations say, "Huh? What?" you can answer, "I'm sorry, Aunt Madge, but it's kind of hard to talk over the TV. Do you think we could turn it down a little, or maybe even turn it off for a while?"

2. **Pretend not to hear what your relations are saying.** (Depending on how loud the TV is, you may not have to pretend.) Say, "I'm sorry, Uncle Doug, but I

---

* For two exceptions to this rule, see page 20.

missed what you just said. Could you turn down the TV a little, or maybe even turn it off for a while? I'd love it if we could just talk."

SPOTLIGHT ON...
SLOPPY KISSERS

You must be irresistible. Otherwise, why would your relatives grab you whenever they see you? They cover you with kisses and you end up with lipstick (or worse) on every square inch of your face.

How can you keep from getting kissed without being rude? It's hard to reject a kiss without hurting or insulting the person offering it. If you can, grin and bear it. Or don't grin. Since the kisser won't see your face, no one will be the wiser.

You can also try sticking out your hand for a handshake. Some relations will use it as a way to pull you closer, but others may take the hint.

Or you could go for an air kiss by turning your cheek.

You might also try saying, "Better not kiss me—I've got a cold. I'd feel terrible if you came down with it, too." Say this every time you see that person and he or she might one day get the message.

Or you could just be up-front and say, "Auntie Jane, how lovely to see you. No, no kisses. I'm getting too old for that. But let me give you a hug."

As a last resort, wear a sign around your neck saying, "Bubonic Plague Carrier."

Thank-You Notes

Why have a chapter on thank-you notes in a book about family manners? Because, when we asked adults, "Which good manners would you most like your kids to have?" their #2 answer was, "Write thank-you notes."

Parents *hate it* when kids don't write thank-you notes. Some parents have been known to hound their kids for years about unwritten notes:

"Maurice, have you written a thank-you note to Aunt Sarah for that sweater she made you?"

"Ma, I got that sweater for Christmas when I was five!"

"Yes, but have you sent her a note?"

"I'm fifteen years old!"

"Well, it's not too late."

To some parents, a telephoned thank-you (even long-distance) doesn't count. Neither does an in-person, face-to-face thank-you. An email thank-you? You've got to be kidding. They want to see The Note.

Yet teenagers stall. They sulk. They procrastinate. They would rather do almost anything than sit down with a pen and a piece of paper, or even a card with "Thank You" already printed on the front.

The reason teenagers have such a hard time writing thank-you notes is because they start off with the wrong attitude. They think of it as a *chore* instead of an *opportunity* to make the gift-giver feel wonderful.

They have forgotten this basic truth: People who feel wonderful are more likely to keep giving you gifts than those who don't.

With that in mind...

Tips for Terrific Thank-You Notes

IF YOU'RE NOT SURE WHETHER TO WRITE A THANK-YOU NOTE, WRITE ONE. It's better to overthank than underthank.

Notes are required for all gifts received by mail, UPS, FedEx, or Pony Express, whether for a birthday, graduation, Bar or Bat Mitzvah, confirmation, Christmas, Chanukah, Kwaanza, Ramadan, etc.

You should also write notes for services rendered, hospitality provided, and thoughtfulnesses extended. ***Examples:***

1. A friend's mother drives you to softball practice twice a week for the whole summer. Of course, you say

thank-you after each ride. But if you also send her a written thank-you note at the end of the summer, she'll think you're the greatest.

2. Your parents go on a business trip during the school year. You can't stay home alone (okay, maybe you *could,* but your parents won't let you), so arrangements are made for you to stay with a neighbor. A written thank-you sent soon after makes you seem even more loveable.

3. You're struggling in math, and your teacher knows it. She offers to stay late two nights a week to tutor you. Written thanks are due, along with your homework.

Generally, you don't have to write notes when people give you presents in person and you thank them verbally. But think of the mileage you could get out of a follow-up note!

WRITE IMMEDIATELY. Thank-you notes get more difficult to write with each day that passes. By the second day, they are *four* times harder to write. By the third day, they are *nine* times harder, and if you wait 12 days, they are *144* times harder to write!

WRITE BY HAND. Thank-you notes should not be typed or written on a computer. Use personal note stationery or attractive cards (the ones that are blank inside). However, if your handwriting is horrid, it's better to send a laser-printed letter than none at all.

NEVER BEGIN WITH "THANK YOU FOR...." Start with some news, a memory of the event or visit, a statement of your friendship, or other charming chitchat.

Example: You've just spent two weeks with the Gump family (distant cousins on your mother's side) at their California seaside condo. You might write:

Dear Mr. and Mrs. Gump

I'm back here in Iowa, safe and sound. School started three days ago, and it already seems as if I've been back for three months. I can't believe it was just last week that I left the sunny shores of the Pacific for the long flight back home.

I can't tell you how much I enjoyed my visit...

Mention the places they took you to, the memories you'll cherish, the delicious dinners, etc. Then, and only then, thank them for their thoughtfulness and generosity. Say you hope that one day you and your parents can host their kid for a stay in America's heartland. You'll bring smiles to the faces of the Gumps, make a fine impression, and guarantee a standing invitation for surf, sun, and fun.

ALWAYS MENTION THE GIFT BY NAME. If I give somebody a wedding present, and I get a letter back that simply thanks me for my "wonderful and generous gift," I know it's a form letter they cranked out. Even if it's handwritten. Make the effort to refer to the gift in some way:

> "All my friends are jealous of my new radio."

> "You must have read my mind to know I wanted fuzzy slippers."

> "I'm absolutely thrilled with my unabridged dictionary."

ALWAYS MENTION SPECIAL MOMENTS. If the gift was one of hospitality, you must send a note, even if you thanked your hosts during the visit. When you write, don't just say, "Thanks for letting me stay with you." Let your hosts know the things that made the visit so special. *Examples:* The time you fell into the river. Being eaten alive by mosquitoes. Having your picture taken with Mickey Mouse.

TELL HOW YOU'RE GOING TO SPEND THE MONEY. If someone gives you the big green, mention what you plan to do with it. If you have no idea, make something up:

> "I'm planning to buy a CD that I've been wanting for ages."

> "I've started saving for a car, and this gives me a real start toward that goal."

DON'T SPOIL YOUR THANKS WITH A BUMMER. Not every gift will be to your liking. Sometimes this is nobody's fault.

Avoid saying things that let gift-givers know their gift wasn't right for you:

"I lost it the first time I took it to school."

"It hit a tree and broke."

"It made me sneeze, so my mom threw it out."

DON'T FORGET TO MAIL YOUR THANK-YOU NOTE. It's shocking how often this happens. Thank-you notes get written, put into envelopes, addressed, stamped, and forgotten. If you find a note you wrote ages ago but never sent, rush it to the mailbox. Check first to make sure the postage is still enough.

Going Far
in the Family Car

The minute you get your driver's license, your mom and dad start to worry—a lot.

They worry that their insurance costs will go sky-high. They worry that you'll get stopped for speeding. They worry that you'll run someone over or have an accident.

They worry that you'll drink and drive, that your friends will drink and drive, or that other drivers will drink and drive, and you'll be hurt or killed.

They worry that you'll spend too much time in the backseat, and you won't be looking for quarters.

In fact, adults have good reason to worry about teen drivers. Motor vehicle accidents are the #1 killer of 16- to

19-year-olds. Forty-four percent of all teens are involved in a crash before their 17th birthday.

Your driving puts your parents' two most precious possessions—you and their car—together in the same place at the same time. This is a constant source of family friction. It will help if you follow certain...

Rules of the Manners Road

NEGOTIATE UP-FRONT. Even before you get your license, impress your parents with how mature you are. Ask them how they'd like to handle insurance, gas, maintenance, reserving the car, whether you can take the car when they aren't around, etc.

CLEAN UP YOUR ACT IN GENERAL. Parents will draw strange connections between, for example, the condition of your room and your driving abilities. They will link your personal habits, your grades, your friends, the music you like, and your appearance to your potential behind-the-wheel behavior:

> "I don't see how you can drive a car if you can't even make your bed in the morning."

> "Some driver you'll be. You left the water running in the sink again."

> "Get a haircut or forget about borrowing the car."

Huh?

It won't make sense, but it will happen. Do what you can to come across as a sane, responsible teen.

DON'T LITTER. Pick up and dispose of all candy wrappers, food, paper bags, and soda cans that you and your friends bring into the car.

TAKE GOOD CARE OF THE CAR. Maybe a mini-van isn't your dream car, but it's better than no car. Without being asked, give it a wash and a vacuum from time to time. Check the tires and fluid levels. Wax it twice a year.

TURN YOUR DRIVING INTO A FAMILY ASSET. Help your parents realize the benefits of having another driver in the family. Offer to do errands that your dad or mom would normally have to do—and make good on your offer.

GIVE YOUR PARENTS GAS. When people hop into a car, they are often in a hurry. They need to get to work, pick someone up, or catch a plane. It's very annoying to find that the previous driver left a thimbleful of fuel in the tank.

So never return the car empty. Fill 'er up. Make an agreement with your parents about who pays. *Examples:* If you use most of a tank for your personal driving, you should pay to fill it. If you use most of a tank for a combination of personal driving and errands for your parents, you can split the costs. If your folks do most of the driving, tell them you'll happily keep the tank topped if they'll keep your funds from running on empty.

Bonus Behaviors

Here are four easy ways to earn extra manners miles:

TURN OFF THE RADIO. Parents have sensitive ears. They don't like to turn the key and get blasted out of their seat by a thousand decibels of hip-hop or garage punk when they were expecting the sweet purr of the engine.

RETURN THE DIAL TO YOUR PARENTS' RADIO STATION. A lot of moms and dads listen to just one favorite station when driving. For some reason, they find it annoying to have to bump those digitals all the way from 106.3 back to 89.7. Restore the dial to the station to which it was tuned. You know—the boring oldies station.

RETURN THE SEAT TO YOUR PARENTS' POSITION. Tiny moms dislike getting into the driver's seat after their 6'4" sons have pushed it all the way back. And 6'4" moms dislike smashing their knees on the steering wheel after their tiny teens have pushed the seat all the way up. Each time you leave the car, return the seat to the approximate position you found it in. If your car has memory buttons for different seat positions, you can return it to the *exact* position preferred by the person most likely to drive it next.

MAKE A SPECIAL EFFORT TO ACT MORE MATURE AT HOME. When your parents agree to let you drive, they're trusting that you're mature enough to handle it. Don't disappoint them. Help reassure them that you won't act like all those rude, impatient, and dangerous so-called ADULTS on the highway.

Making Your Way Down the Highway

Once you get behind the wheel, new rules come into effect. The rules of the road. Or, more accurately, the rules of the jungle. For that's what it's like out there.

Some of the rudest of all human behavior happens behind the wheel of a car. There's no stopping the ME FIRST! mentality when it's reinforced by 4,000 pounds of steel. People feel anonymous and protected when driving. They do things they wouldn't dare to do at other times.

Take tailgating, for example. Drivers think nothing of roaring down the highway at 60 miles per hour two inches behind the car in front of them. But they wouldn't dream of walking down the sidewalk two inches behind another pedestrian.

Or how about honking. If some poor guy doesn't burn rubber within .000001 seconds of the light turning green, the Very Important Person behind him blasts him out of his seat with a

HONK!!!!

Can you imagine being in line to buy concert tickets and having the person behind you scream in your ear

GET GOING!!!
CAN'T YOU SEE THE LINE HAS MOVED?!!

Neither can I.

There are at least three reasons for you to drive politely:

1. so your parents will trust you with the car

2. so you'll be a safe driver

3. so you won't get chased by a motorist you've ticked off

Use common courtesy when you're in the driver's seat. You're not the only person on the road. Meanwhile, learn everything you can about defensive driving techniques. Learn how to drive in snow and wet weather. Get a patient adult with nerves of steel to practice with you. Afterward, send him or her a thank-you note.

16 COMMANDMENTS
OF DRIVER'S ETIQUETTE

THOU SHALT...

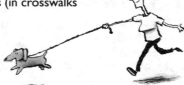

1. stop for pedestrians (in crosswalks and on jaywalks)

2. yield the right of way when you don't have it

3. yield the right of way when you *do* have it, but that truck looks awfully serious

4. keep the radio volume low enough to hear other cars, emergency vehicles, etc.

5. in heavy traffic, wave someone in who'd otherwise be stuck forever*

6. always wear your seat belt and insist that your passengers do, too

7. use your turn signals

8. leave a note with your name and phone number if you hit a parked car

---

*You'll get where you're going .002 seconds later than you would have otherwise, but the look of amazement on the person's face, and the warm glow in your heart, will more than make up for it.

continues...

16 COMMANDMENTS
OF DRIVER'S ETIQUETTE

THOU SHALT NOT...

9. aim for pedestrians

10. run anyone over (this is *very* bad manners)

11. tailgate

12. talk on your cell phone while driving**

13. hog the passing lane***

14. take up two spots in a parking lot

15. open your car door into the vehicle parked next to you

16. drink and drive

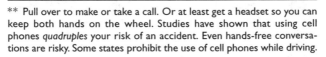

** Pull over to make or take a call. Or at least get a headset so you can keep both hands on the wheel. Studies have shown that using cell phones *quadruples* your risk of an accident. Even hands-free conversations are risky. Some states prohibit the use of cell phones while driving.

*** On multilane freeways, use the right-hand lane for cruising, the left-hand lane for passing. Hogging the passing lane is one of the rudest, most dangerous things a driver can do. In Europe, nobody would dream of doing this. A car going slowly in the passing lane would be eaten by a Ferrari doing 150 m.p.h. But here in America, people dawdle along at 40 and refuse to pull over.

When Parents Are Rude

Strangers, nonrelatives, and casual acquaintances aren't the only adults who are rude to children and teenagers. Parents—maybe including *your* parents—can be shockingly rude.

This may have to do with the confusion between "company manners" and "being real." Or it may be linked to the mistaken belief that honesty is always the best policy. (More about that in a moment.) Whatever the cause, rude parents are as offensive as rude kids.

Coping with Criticism

When parents are rude, it's usually in the area of criticizing their children. True, some criticism is deserved. When criticism is constructive, it can even be welcome. But criticism is bad manners when it's destructive, petty, or mean. ***Example:*** There's no excuse for a parent who says, "Can't you do anything right?" when he or she could say, "Let me show you how I learned to do that."

Often, the problem is one of definitions. It seems that parents and children use different dictionaries when it comes to defining behavior:

What parents call...	**Children call...**
guidance	criticism
reminding	nagging
for your own good	totally unfair
ignoring	forgetting
slamming	shutting

 The next time your parents criticize you, try saying, "You're absolutely right. I'm sorry. I'll try to do better." This stops criticism dead in its tracks. I guarantee it.

20 Rude Things Parents Say to Teenagers

• •

When we asked teens, "What are the rudest things your parents have ever said to you?" these were among their answers:

1. "How can you be so dumb?"

2. "You don't try hard enough."

3. "What's wrong with you?"

4. "You little @$#!%&!"

5. "Don't you ever think?"

6. "You'll never amount to anything."

7. "You should have known better."

8. "You're wearing *that* to school?"

9. "Get over here."

10. "Get off the phone."

11. "Get out of my sight."

12. "Go to your room."

13. "Do what I say."

14. "Don't cry or I'll hit you even harder."

15. "I don't believe you."

16. "I can't wait for you to leave home."

17. "Why can't you be like so-and-so?"

18. "If so-and-so jumped off a bridge, would you?"

19. "Because I said so."

20. "You're too young to understand."

Obviously, you can't *make* your parents be more polite. Parents don't like it when kids try to correct their behavior. Once again, they use different dictionaries:

When children say...	Parents hear...
"Please don't embarrass me in front of my friends."	children who are being bossy
"Please don't shout at me."	children who are out of line
"Please don't call me names."	children who are asking for trouble
"That's not fair."	children who have forgotten who's in charge

So, what can you do when your parents are rude? You can set a good example by being more polite. Even when you're frustrated, and even when you're angry. Think before you speak, and maybe your parents will learn from you and do the same.

20 Rude Things Teenagers Say to Parents

When we asked parents, "What are the rudest things your children have ever said to you?" these were among their answers:

1. "Leave me alone."

2. "Mind your own business."

3. "Get out of my face."

4. "Get out of my life."

5. "Stay out of my room."

6. "Shut up."

7. "@$#!%&! you!"

8. "I wish you weren't my mother/father."

9. "I wish I was never born."

10. "I wish you were dead."

11. "I hate being part of this family."

12. "You don't own me."

13. "You can't tell me what to do."

14. "I'll do what I want."

15. "You can't make me."

16. "You never do anything for me."

17. "You're a nag."

18. "It's my life."

19. "Who says?"

20. "You're too old to understand."

Is Honesty Always the Best Policy?

One of the first lessons parents teach their children is, "You must never tell a lie." Soon after, a neighbor comes to visit. Mommy says, "Would you like to give Mrs. Sweetums a kiss?" And little Johnny, remembering his parents' advice, says, "No! She's ugly and smells bad."

As soon as Mrs. Sweetums is out the door, Johnny learns the second lesson parents teach their children: "You must never tell a lie, but you must not always tell the truth." The parent then explains that there's a difference between *lying to stay out of trouble* (which is bad) and *lying to avoid hurting someone's feelings* (which can be good).

Knowing when to tell the truth and when to take creative liberties is at the heart of good manners. Because this issue is so important, we wanted to learn what teenagers thought about it. So we asked them, "Is honesty always the best policy?"

Here's what the teenagers we surveyed said:

YES it is	39%
NO it isn't	61%

And here are some reasons they gave:

"HONESTY IS ALWAYS THE BEST POLICY BECAUSE..."

"If you're honest, your parents will trust you."

"When you're honest, you never have to remember any lies."

"If you're not honest, it will eventually come back to you in a bad way."

"If you lie, you always get found out, and then you get in trouble for lying AND for doing the thing you lied about."

In the words of one wise teen:

"Honesty is the best policy. But it's not always the most convenient policy."

"HONESTY ISN'T ALWAYS THE BEST POLICY BECAUSE..."

Some teenagers saw lying as a way to avoid hassles:

"You can get away with things when you don't tell the truth."

"Honesty isn't the best policy—at least, not with parents."

"Honesty may get you into more trouble than you need."

"If the other person will never know the difference and the truth will hurt you, zip your lip."

Others saw lying as a way to prevent hurt feelings:

"When giving opinions, lying is better than criticizing."

"I wouldn't want to tell someone they're ugly or look nasty."

"Honesty can sometimes make people commit suicide, cry, get hurt emotionally, or want revenge on you."

"Telling someone EXACTLY what you think is never good."

So, is honesty always the best policy or not? The answer is, "It depends."

The teenagers who said "Yes" realized that telling the truth leads to self-respect, a clear conscience, and the trust of others. They were aware that lies can trip you up and get you into trouble. They were looking at the issue from the *moral* angle.

Most teenagers who said "No" were looking at it from the *manners* angle. They knew that there are situations where telling the truth can be cruel, upsetting, and pointless.

This doesn't mean that it's okay to lie. It means that it's sometimes okay to substitute good manners for the literal truth. Here are a few examples:

- You're feeling lonely and sad and you have a stomachache. A friend of your mother's drops by the house and asks, "How are you?" You say, "Fine, thanks." This isn't a lie, even though it's not the truth. You understood that the friend was just being polite, not really asking about your health.

- You have dinner at a friend's house. The food tastes so bad you can barely get it down. When it's time to leave, you say, "Thank you so much for having me over for dinner. I really enjoyed it." You don't say, "Your cooking was terrible and I almost threw up." This is because you're not a food critic. You're a sensitive human being who wishes to thank people for being kind to you, even if they can't cook.

- A classmate invites you to a dance. What goes through your mind is, "I think you're gross and dull, and I wouldn't be caught dead at a dance with you." What comes out of your mouth is, "I'm sorry, but I already have plans." Even if you don't. This is because the question being asked is, "Will you go out with me?" and not, "What do you think of me?"

What are you supposed to say when someone asks you if they look fat?

You say, "Certainly not! Whatever gave you that idea?"

People who ask this question are looking for reassurance, not honesty. They're saying, "Please help me to feel okay about myself."

It's important to be able to recognize questions like these when you hear them. Sometimes they're disguised as statements ("I look so fat!"). And sometimes they're introduced with, "Now, I want your honest opinion...." But don't be fooled. The last thing the person wants is your honest opinion.

Since these questions are often asked by our closest friends and loved ones, you need to know what to say when the trap is laid. Here are some practice questions. For each one, pick the answer you think is best:

"Do I look all right?"
a) "That depends on what you consider all right."
b) "You look terrific."

"Is my hair okay?"
a) "It is if you're a rat looking for a nest."
b) "Your hair is fine."

"I messed up so bad in my piano recital!"
a) "I'll say. Thirty people walked out."
b) "Oh, no. It sounded wonderful."

In every example, the proper answer is b. But you knew that. ◆

What Are Manners, Anyway?

Manners are customs and traditions that guide how people treat each other and behave in social situations.

Manners are meant to smooth the rough edges of human nature. They maintain order, promote a society's values, and encourage positive human interactions.

Imagine the chaos and hurt we would experience if everybody did whatever they wanted, whenever they wanted, without any regard for the feelings or interests of others.

MANNERS CAN VARY FROM ONE CULTURE TO ANOTHER. In Japan, you would remove your shoes before entering some-one's house. If you did this in America, people would give you strange looks and hold their noses. In some Asian and Middle Eastern countries, belching and smacking your lips is a way to compliment the chef. In the United States, it's a way to get sent to your room.

IT'S IMPORTANT TO KNOW THE MANNERS OF THE CULTURE YOU'RE IN. Otherwise, an innocent, friendly gesture could cause offense or embarrassment. *Examples:* In Australia, an enthusiastic thumbs-up sign doesn't mean "All riiiiiight!" It means "Up yours!" Latinos, Asians, and people in Middle Eastern and Mediterranean countries see same-sex hand-holding as a sign of friendship. In America, many people would assume it means you're gay.

MANNERS ARE CONSTANTLY CHANGING. *Examples:* Children in Western cultures no longer bow or curtsy when pre-sented to adults. Women today do things—drive, pick up the tab, wear bikinis—that would have been shocking 100 years ago. Some manners are almost extinct (how a lady should enter a horse-drawn carriage) while others are rela-tively young and new (how to send email).

DIFFERENT SUBCULTURES HAVE THEIR OWN UNIQUE MANNERS. Think surfers, bikers, teenagers, business executives, sena-tors, musicians, women, men, ethnic groups, etc. You prob-ably act differently around your friends than you do around your boss, if you have a job. People with good manners are sensitive to their surroundings. They adapt their behavior accordingly.

SOMETIMES MANNERS NEED ADJUSTING ON THE SPOT.
Example: You've invited a date to a movie. At the theater, you start to pay for both tickets. She (or he) protests. You insist. She (or he) protests some more. At some point, it's more polite for each of you to pay for your own ticket.

Finally: You may have heard that the purpose of manners is to make people feel comfortable. That's very true. But sometimes—and here's where being polite can be so much fun—the purpose of manners is to make people *uncomfortable!* **Examples:** Someone makes a racial slur. You get to say, "Excuse me? I must not have heard you correctly. You couldn't have said what I thought you said!" Or someone invades your private life. You get to say, "Pardon me? Do we know each other well enough for you to ask me that?"

Being courteous doesn't mean letting people walk all over you. Sometimes, those who are unkind and inconsiderate need to be put in their place—politely, of course.

Is It Ever Okay Not to Have Good Manners?

Yes. You're excused from having good manners if...

1. you're too young to know better

2. you have a physical or mental illness that prevents you from having the necessary self-awareness or control

3. it's an emergency (firefighters don't have to say "Excuse me" as they brush past bystanders blocking their path)

4. you're a crime victim (introductions aren't necessary when being mugged)

5. you're alone and your actions don't have negative consequences for anyone else (***Example:*** it's okay to eat whipped cream from the can in the privacy of your own bedroom—just don't put the can back in the refrigerator)

6. you're with other people, and you all agree to suspend certain manners for the time being—as long as this doesn't have negative consequences for anyone else (***Example:*** it's okay to burp loudly while watching football and eating junk food with your friends)

Are there any more reasons not to have good manners?

No. ◆

INDEX

ABOUT THE AUTHOR

Alex J. Packer (but you may call him "Alex") is a very polite educator and psychologist who only drinks from the carton if nobody's watching. He is the author of the award-winning *How Rude!™ The Teenagers' Guide to Good Manners, Proper Behavior, and Not Grossing People Out; HIGHS! Over 150 Ways to Feel Really, REALLY Good... Without Alcohol or Other Drugs; Bringing Up Parents: The Teenager's Handbook; Parenting One Day at a Time;* and other titles. His books have been translated into Spanish, German, and Chinese, although Alex says he can't tell if the Chinese version is really his book or a guide to lawnmower repair. His articles have appeared in *McCall's, Child, U.S. News and World Report,* and the *Harvard Graduate School of Education Bulletin.*

Alex prepped at Phillips Exeter Academy, where he never once referred to kitchen personnel as "wombats" (although he *was* told to get a haircut by his dorm master). He then went to Harvard, where he pursued a joint major in Social Relations and Finger Bowls, always striving to avoid classes on Mondays or Fridays. A specialist in adolescence, parent education, and substance abuse, Alex received a Master's Degree in Education from the Harvard Graduate School of (duh) Education, and a Ph.D. in Educational and Developmental Psychology from Boston College, where he held doors for his professors.

For eight years, Alex was headmaster of an alternative school for children ages 11–15 in Washington, D.C. He has since served as Director of Education for the Capital Children's Museum. He is currently President of FCD Educational Services, a leading Boston-based provider of drug education and prevention services for schools worldwide. When asking kids to not use drugs, Alex always says "please."

Although it's rude to talk behind someone's back, reliable sources report that Alex writes screenplays, spends several months a year in France, lives in a loft that used to be a pillow factory, and chews with his mouth closed.

Other Great Books from Free Spirit

How Rude!™
The Teenagers' Guide to Good Manners,
Proper Behavior, and Not Grossing People Out
by Alex J. Packer, Ph.D.
Fourteen chapters describe the basics
of polite behavior at home, in school,
and in the world. Teens learn how to be
a host with the most (and a guest with
the best), what to do (and not to do)
when going online or waiting in line,
how to act at the mall and a concert
hall, and much more. For ages 13 & up.
$19.95; 480 pp.; softcover; illus.; 7¼" x 9"

The How Rude!™ Handbook of
School Manners for Teens
by Alex J. Packer, Ph.D.
What counts as rude behavior in school? When
someone tries to copy off of your paper during
tests, should you rat or not? How can you dress
for school success? What's the best way to
handle bullies, bigots, bashers, and harassers?
School can be cruel. Here's sound advice
(touched with humor) for teens who want to
make it more bearable. For ages 13 & up.
$9.95; 128 pp.; softcover; illus.; 5⅛" x 7"

The How Rude!™ Handbook of
Friendship & Dating Manners for Teens
by Alex J. Packer, Ph.D.
Is there a proper way to make new friends? Is
teasing always rude? How can you show a girl
(or guy) that you like her (or him)? What's the best
way to ask someone out...and who pays for the
date? This book answers these questions and
more. Teens learn the basics of polite behavior
with friends and more-than-friends—and laugh
out loud while learning. For ages 13 & up.
$9.95; 128 pp.; softcover; illus.; 5⅛" x 7"